MW00422785

Birds
of
Lake
Merritt

Birds of Lake Merritt

Alex Harris

Heyday, Berkeley, California

Library of Congress Cataloging-in-Publication Data

Names: Harris, Alex, 1983- author, illustrator.
Title: Birds of Lake Merritt / Alex Harris.
Description: Berkeley, California : Heyday, 2021. | Includes
   bibliographical references.
Identifiers: LCCN 2021010506 (print) | LCCN 2021010507 (ebook) | ISBN
   9781597145480 (board) | ISBN 9781597145619 (epub)
Subjects: LCSH: Water birds--California--Merritt, Lake--Identification.
Classification: LCC QL678.5 .H37 2021 (print) | LCC QL678.5 (ebook)
| DDC
   598.17609794/66--dc23
LC record available at https://lccn.loc.gov/2021010506
LC ebook record available at https://lccn.loc.gov/2021010507

Cover Art: Alex Harris
Cover Design: Ashley Ingram
Interior Design/Typesetting: Ashley Ingram

Published by Heyday
P.O. Box 9145, Berkeley, California 94709
(510) 549-3564
heydaybooks.com

Printed in East Peoria, Illinois, by Versa Press, Inc.

FSC
www.fsc.org
MIX
Paper from
responsible sources
FSC® C005010

10 9 8 7 6 5 4 3 2 1

Dedicated to my family—thanks for everything

Contents

Acknowledgments

Thanks and appreciation to all who gave their time and attention to this book.

Allie for her endless support.

Natalie Jones, Nina Lewallen Hufford, L. John Harris, Alec Scott, Lynn Schofield, Michele D. Jones, and Marthine Satris for editing.

Ashley Ingram and Diane Lee for making everything look good.

Heyday, for having me.

Everyone who contributed their words or shared their experiences with me: Timbo, Jenny Odell, Rue Mapp, Cindy Margulis, Clayton Anderson. My dad for always encouraging my artistic endeavors. The Oakland Library, Walden Pond, and Spectator Books for books and source materials. Corrina and Deja Gould for fact checking and editing the Ohlone history. Julian Marszalek and Nina Mae Haggerty for general support and discussion. Sally for teaching me how to draw, Ajene for inspiration, and Maria Schoettler and Leah Tumerman for artistic encouragement. David Weidenfeld for his love of books. Those who did all the hard work of developing the historical, scientific, and cultural knowledge that this book drew upon.

ROTARY NATURE CENTER

GRAND AVE

THE PERGOLA

ADAMS POINT

BIRD ISLANDS

LAKESIDE DRIVE

LAKESHORE AVENUE

LAKE MERRITT

ABOUT WHERE THE DAM WAS

CHANNEL TO THE ESTUARY AND THEN THE BAY AND THEN THE OCEAN

Introduction

Lake Merritt has been called the heart of the city of Oakland, as well as its lungs. It is the "crown jewel" of Oakland, and said to be draped in a necklace of lights. Surrounded by parks and gardens, with the buildings of the city just beyond, the lake is at once at the center of the city and a welcome respite from it. People stroll along the scenic paved pathways, row across the glistening waters, and admire the city skyline while picnicking along the verdant ring of parkland surrounding it. Often, this grassy green oasis is dotted with goose poop. Along with the people, there are flocks of geese at the lake. They swim in the water, stand obstinately in the way of joggers, and nibble on the grass. There are many other birds who frequent the lake as well: ducks, herons, egrets, pelicans, grebes, cormorants, coots—and those are just the ones in the water; many other species live in the surrounding trees and gardens. But what are these birds doing in the middle of the city, and why do the residents of Oakland tolerate so much goose poop?

My interest in answering these questions began when I attempted to learn how to identify the various species of hawk that one might see in California by painting them, bird by bird, and at the same time get better at painting. Surely, spending ten hours painting a bird would help me to better understand gouache and watercolor, as well as enable me to differentiate between a Red-tailed and Cooper's Hawk. Two birds with one stone. I found beautiful photographs of these birds and painted them as best I could. The paintings turned out fine, but what I failed to account for was that rarely, in day-to-day life, do you encounter hawks that are ten feet away, standing perfectly still on a fence post and staring straight at you, as many photographs of hawks would have you believe. It turns out that you mostly see hawks from beneath, hundreds of feet away, a blurred silhouette circling in the skies above. Painting from photographs had not prepared me for this. I decided that I should look a little closer to home, so I rode my bike over to the bird sanctuary at Lake Merritt.

While I watched the ducks at the lake, I came across the then-shuttered Rotary Nature Center, which piqued my interest. I soon learned that Lake Merritt was the first wildlife refuge in the nation. Right here, in Oakland! I grew up in Berkeley, spent my teenage years exploring every nook and cranny of the East Bay (or so I thought), and even got a degree in environmental studies, but had no idea about this piece of important local environmental history. A trip to the Oakland History Room at the nearby library sent me on my way toward understanding the history of the wildlife refuge at Lake Merritt.

One hundred and fifty years ago, Samuel Merritt, a wealthy landowner and the mayor of Oakland, asked the State of California to ban bird hunting in the tidal estuary on the outskirts of the new city, and thus to create the first officially recognized wildlife refuge in the United States. The statute, passed on March 18, 1870, read: "It shall be unlawful for any person to take, kill or destroy, in any manner whatever, any grouse, any species of wild duck, crane, heron, swan, pelican, snipe or any wild animal or game, of any kind or species whatever, upon, in or around Lake Merritt." And with that, the birds were now free to exist on the water and in the wetlands undisturbed—to rest, hunt, raise families, and fertilize the lawns, and neighbors and visitors could observe them as they did.

But why look at birds? As an artist and nature-interested person, I think birds are cool to look at for their natural forms and traits: the alien technology of a coot's foot, the cormorant's dinosaur-like crooked neck, the complex colors of a duck. But birds also serve as a daily reminder that we humans are not the only ones here on this planet. As John Berger writes in the 1977 essay "Why Look at Animals?": "With

"This space reserved for the ducks. Please keep out" (William L. Finley, 1920, courtesy of the Oregon Historical Society).

their parallel lives, animals offer man a companionship which is different from any offered by human exchange. Different because it is a companionship offered to the loneliness of man as a species." Today, the wildlife refuge at Lake Merritt provides both the experience of marveling at the beauty of the birds' variety of form and color and also a reminder that we are part of a large, complicated, beautiful world.

In many ways, the history of Lake Merritt traces, and in some instances portends, the dawn of the broader environmental movement in the US. An appreciation of nature for its own sake was not common at the time of the refuge's founding, and even less so the intentional preservation of it. Open spaces in cities constructed around this time—such as Central Park in New York City and Golden Gate Park—were generally for city residents' recreation, not for the conservation of natural spaces and wild creatures. Merritt's advocacy for the birds at the edge of Oakland was part of a burgeoning national reckoning with the effects of widespread bird hunting, just as Audubon societies were forming in response to the use of feathers in fashionable hats. As the tide turned, the first national park, Yellowstone, would be established just a few years after Lake Merritt's designation as a refuge.

Like the broader environmental movement at the time, the refuge at Lake Merritt was, at least initially, predominantly the province of wealthy residents, and was not intended as any sort of public park. Indeed, the land that bordered the lake's marshy edges was private. Those who wished to sail on it could rent boats from the landowners who owned boathouses along its banks. "Nature" was a privilege to be enjoyed by those with the time and resources to access and experience it. This version of nature was understood to be a pure thing, away from streets, buildings, and the masses, in fact defined by this separation. These sentiments were perhaps most prominently conveyed in the writing of famed naturalist John Muir, founder of the Sierra Club, who wrote zealously of the importance of escaping civilization to spend time in the mountains (often a tall task for those with jobs, families, and responsibilities at home).

Here, though, Lake Merritt eventually went against the grain, and its very existence has proven this older view of nature and wildness to be a narrow one. Rex Burress, one of the early lead naturalists at the Rotary Nature Center, the interpretive center at Lake Merritt, wrote a piece for *California Parks and Recreation* magazine in 1962 titled "Letter to John Muir," in which he confronts Muir's vision of a stark division between "nature" and "not nature":

> This would surprise you, but right here in the heart of Oakland by Lake Merritt, there is a bird refuge where wild ducks and geese will eat out of your hand!! Wild pintails and canvasbacks and bluebills and a host of other free flying birds that have swooped over the Sierras— looking down on the most rugged of wilderness areas— come to this refuge where they dwell with city and man in sweet accord. And this is a goal to strive for; the merger of man and nature. And it must be if we are to keep burning before us the hopeful light of scenes from the world of nature. There is no need to make our cities a tomb of machines, because man *can* merge with nature and make a place practical for wild things and beautiful for homes.

Perhaps it is no longer a radical idea that there is validity in the nature that we find all around us in the city. Backyard bird feeders, bee-friendly gardens, neighborhood nature walks—all speak to the general acceptance that not only is nature all around but that we are, or at least can be, active participants in it. Burress and his contemporaries gave the Rotary Nature Center the unofficial motto "Toward bringing nature and people together," and it would seem that, to a large extent, they have been successful.

Lake It or Not

Although we call it a lake, Lake Merritt is, generally speaking, a tidal wetland—shallow land covered permanently or periodically by water. It is also an estuary, where freshwater meets the sea. It is also a slough, a narrow and slow-moving section of an inlet or creek. It is a lagoon. It is a mudflat. Spanish settlers called it Lake Peralta, but after Samuel Merritt dammed the body of water around 1868, it really started to resemble a lake, and early Oaklanders started to call it Lake Merritt. The name stuck like a boot in mud.

But how correct is it to call Lake Merritt a "lake"? A lake is a body of water large enough to be considered a geographic feature, which Lake Merritt surely is, but also one separate from the ocean, which Lake Merritt is not. So, failing one of the two conditions, Lake Merritt is not technically a lake. But perhaps a lake can be more of a state of mind: in her contribution to the book *Home Ground: A Guide to the American Landscape*, Patricia Hampl makes the case that a lake is "both a place and a condition." If Oaklanders treat Lake Merritt like a lake, and if it looks like a lake (and quacks like a lake), then isn't Lake Merritt a lake?

Before it resembled a lake at all, however, the slough where Lake Merritt now lies would, at low tide, reveal hundreds of acres of marsh, a liminal landscape of rushes and mudflats, sheltering species that specialized in brackish living. To get a sense of what it would have looked like, just take a trip to some of the extant wetlands in the Bay Area, such as at the San Pablo Bay National Wildlife Refuge near Vallejo. Now squint and pretend you are in downtown Oakland. This type of terrain, a jigsaw puzzle of reeds, water, and mud, is what much of the San Francisco Bay looked like at one point, with around 190,000 acres of wetlands surrounding it. Although the muckiness of these areas, neither land nor water, might have once kept them safe from destruction, they have been mostly paved over, filled in, and built on over the last 150 years. Today, only about 15 percent of the bay's original wetlands remain.

Prior to being paved over, these wetlands, a treasure trove of biodiversity, made San Francisco Bay a popular destination for birds along the Pacific Flyway, one of four highway-like routes in the sky that birds use to traverse the Americas as they migrate north and south with the seasons. Wetlands along the flyways provide birds with easily accessible food and a place to rest. It is as if drive-thrus along the highway served free bugs, small marine animals, and little bits of plant matter. These restaurants just happen to be self-serve, and the buffet tables are built of vast fields of mud and saltwater. For birds, such an offering is hard to pass up. Reports from before we filled in and paved over the bay shore describe vast numbers of birds populating these areas—the birds flying overhead would darken the sky like a massive cloud and, upon landing, cover the land like an immense blanket.

Before Oakland

The first people to inhabit this land, starting many thousands of years ago and continuing to this day, were the Chochenyo-speaking Ohlone people. Lake Merritt is in an area called Huchiun, which includes everything from Oakland and Alameda north through Albany. During a celebration of the 150th anniversary of the wildlife refuge at Lake Merritt, held in September 2020, Corrina Gould, the tribal spokesperson for the Confederated Villages of Lisjan, summarized how the Ohlone people lived around Lake Merritt up until a few hundred years ago:

> This is a place that my ancestors have been since the beginning of time. A time ago, before other people came here, and this was created into a lake, it was a marsh land.

And my ancestors had village sites that dotted around the different places on the lake, where we were fishermen and used the tule to create our houses, our boats, skirts, many other things. And this was a place of abundance.

The Spanish, who arrived in 1769, forced these Ohlone people to relocate from Huchiun to nearby missions, where they were met by disease, violence, and enslavement. The land they were forced from, which the Spanish called Rancho San Antonio, was given by the crown in 1820 to a soldier named Sergeant Luis María Peralta in payment for over forty years of service in the Spanish army. This 45,000-acre parcel included the Oakland estuary, which the Spanish called San Antonio Creek, and the slough then known as Laguna Peralta, which would become Lake Merritt.

Rancho San Antonio was one of many California land grants made by the Spanish crown. Environmental destruction was common on these ranchos, with livestock overgrazing, extensive agriculture, and hunting decimating native plant populations and local ecologies throughout California. It is possible that Laguna Peralta, muddy tidal marshland that it was, was not of much productive use for agriculture or grazing and was thus saved from the brunt of the environmental impacts of the rancho system.

With the discovery of gold in the Sierra foothills in 1848, people from around the world started flooding into California, mostly arriving in San Francisco and then traveling through the East Bay to the Sierra foothills. New arrivals were here with one primary goal: striking it rich. And while it soon became clear that their chances of hitting the mother lode were not great, California offered other ways to get rich quick. Soon, people were pursuing many of California's other natural resources with the same frenzied Gold Rush fervor. One of these natural resources was wildlife: many of the bird species that can be seen at Lake Merritt today, such as geese, ducks, grebes, and egrets, were hunted in huge quantities. These birds were sold to markets to feed the masses of new arrivals, and some were also prized for their fashionable feathers.

First Avenue along Lake Merritt, circa 1880.

Bird hunting continued in the estuary as a group of failed prospectors wrested control of the land from the Peraltas through a series of dubious, and perhaps intentionally duplicitous, real estate deals, and started building the city of Oakland.

The Nation's First Wildlife Refuge

Shortly after Oakland's incorporation in 1852, a Swiss engineer named Julius Kellersberger was hired by Oakland's founders to design the city's street grid, which stretched from the waterfront at Jack London Square north to where 14th Street is now. Whether intentionally or by oversight, Kellersberger's initial plan did not focus on how to develop the land immediately adjacent to the water, either along what is now Lake Merritt or what is now Jack London Square, and as a result this land was left untouched. Again, the wetlands' inaccessibility and muddy, interstitial nature may have spared it from the brunt of ecological destruction.

The lack of development along the slough was appealing to an ambitious physician and businessman from Maine named Samuel Merritt, who had fallen for that patch of land (and water) on his very first visit:

> I first came to Oakland in 1851 in an open boat, on Sunday, with a party of ladies and gentlemen with lunch baskets. We came down to the water near what is now Lake Merritt. It was in the spring. The grass was green, wild flowers aplenty and the estuary full of ducks. I got into a tree whose branches drooped into the water, and I thought it was the most beautiful sight in the world.

A few years later, in 1854, after many subsequent trips to Oakland, Merritt bought the land stretching from 14th Street to the north arm of the lake for $6,000. He built himself a fine house on the east side of Jackson Street (his house featured the first elevator installed in Oakland) and subsequently built and sold nice big houses with beautiful gardens on the other plots he owned, turning a tidy profit. In 1868, he had the dam built that would turn the tidal estuary into a lake, which he correctly envisioned as an eventual point of great civic pride (and a boost to the value of his real estate).

While Merritt dreamed of an idyllic lake, the shores along his land were still popular with hunters. Upon the refuge's centenary, John V. Young of the *New York Times* would describe the hunting scene at Lake Merritt as a rather unruly affair:

> Some hunters were blasting everything in sight for meat, even robins. Millinery hunters shot any bird with plumes or bright feathers for milady's bonnet. Men and boys shot anything that moved, in the name of sport; it was the spirit of the times.

This free-for-all fracas was interrupting the mayor's regular lakeside walks, and the stray bullets were ending up everywhere, including in a neighbor's cow, according to one oft-recounted tale of this time. As Young describes, "Hunters were peppering residences, and even Sunday picnickers, with stray shot."

The mayor and his neighbors, in a NIMBY-esque pique, grew weary of these lakeside interlopers. Taking full advantage of his connections, the mayor convinced a state senator to introduce a bill in the California legislature making hunting at the lake illegal. In 1870, the state legislature declared Lake Merritt a wildlife refuge, making it the first of its kind in the nation.

While Merritt was no doubt a fan of the ducks—who isn't?—he also had a financial interest in banning hunting. Like damming the lake, eliminating hunting encouraged development and increased the value of the land. This is not something that is evident only in hindsight: consensus among the people of the time was that any improvements to the lake were good for society, and if Merritt happened to personally benefit from them, good for him.

So while the hunting ban was good for Merritt's bottom line, the creation of a wildlife refuge was, at risk of stating the obvious, also good for the wildlife. It isn't hard to imagine that without protections in place, Oakland's local and visiting bird populations would have dwindled further, faster, and irretrievably, as happened to many species in North America during the nineteenth century. The Passenger Pigeon is a stark example of the attitude toward hunting and conservation at the time: once widely abundant, with an estimated North American population of somewhere between three and five billion, by the early twentieth century the pigeon was brought to extinction by hunting and trapping. The Passenger Pigeon saw its most precipitous population decline starting in 1870, coincidentally the same year that hunting was banned at Lake Merritt. By contrast, the Snowy Egret population was also nearly destroyed by hunters in the late 1800s, but has since recovered thanks to protections against hunting and habitat loss. These days, the sun in Oakland isn't blocked out by ducks as it once might have been, but there are still steady populations of both full-time occupants and seasonal visitors. These lucky ducks (and herons and the rest) dodged a bullet with the establishment of the refuge.

A Place for People

While the ducks floated quietly on the water's placid surface, and herons and egrets stilted around the muddy edges, humans continued building Oakland. The people of the time were, unsurprisingly, mostly concerned with their own affairs, and not those of the birds. In the city's early years, the conservation movement in the US was just getting started. Environmentalism, the ideology and social movement as we understand it today, did not exist, and Samuel Merritt's ban on hunting did nothing to address the preservation of the land itself, only forbade the hunting of birds.

Not only were the wetlands not protected by the new law, they weren't even public land. Wealthy citizens such as Merritt owned the land around the lake, and in 1887 it was discovered that the Southern Pacific Railroad owned the actual lake. (Even railroad companies can lose track sometimes.) One of the owners of the railroad wanted to fill in the lake and build a train station. Leland Stanford, a partner in the railroad company and founder of Stanford University, along with Oakland mayor M. C. Chapman, convinced him instead to give the lake to the city. The city acquired the lake in 1891 on the condition that Oakland turn the land around it into a public park.

Keeping the lake a lake would prove to be a fruitful decision for the people of the burgeoning city of Oakland. Lake Merritt, now safe from both hunting and industry, became a great point of civic pride. The editors of the *Oakland Tribune*, a reliable booster of the young city, wrote in 1887:

> Oakland today is classed among the handsomest cities in the U.S.; and when it shall have constructed her grand boulevard around the beautiful lake, which like a lovely pearl in a rich setting, occupies a romantic place in the very heart of the city, together with the contemplated park, stretching away toward Piedmont, constructed by the hand of nature itself, as the necessary lungs of a great city, with romantic glens, rolling hills, sightly and picturesque, it will then boast of a beauty and attractiveness unequalled by any city on the globe.

The "contemplated park," with a boulevard around it, would soon be included in a plan solicited by the city in 1905. The plan was influenced by the nascent nationwide City Beautiful movement, which purported to enhance the moral and civic virtue of city dwellers through urban planning and beautification. The plan focused on how the lake could benefit the humans who lived there, rather than recognizing the lake, and its avian denizens, as having their own merit.

Making Lake Merritt a pleasant place to promenade faced a complication: the city was using the lake as a sewer. Since Oakland's origins, lakeside residents had been directing sewage into what were then tidal flats, whose tides would "flush" the refuse into the bay. As the population grew, the first sewer was built in 1864; ten years later, a system of sixty miles of rudimentary pipes, made of brick and wood,

Looking toward the hills from the 12th Street dam in the 1890s.

was constructed to skirt what had now become a lake, and send the city's waste into the slough beyond the dam. Although this might have seemed a clever solution to a difficult problem (in 1877, the *Oakland Tribune* called it "without exception, the most perfect sewerage main in the world, no other city having such natural facilities"), it was eventually deemed a failure. The sewers leaked, and residents were still dumping their waste directly into the lake. Thanks to the dam, they had created a toilet that couldn't flush. The issue remained until the 1890s with the completion of an improved sewer system that piped sewage straight into the bay.

The dam also caused silt from the lake's freshwater tributaries to build up at its bottom, which then had to be dredged. The material from the dredging had to go somewhere, so it was dumped on the slough's marshy edges. Although this infill disrupted a precious ecosystem, it provided a stable foundation for a new boulevard along the eastern side of the lake (what is now Lakeshore Avenue). Whether this was an intended effect of damming or not, the result was a profound change to the topographic composition of the waterway.

With the ownership confusion and sewage problem resolved, and the wetlands filled in, the stage was set for rapid advances in the development of the land around the lake. In 1907, the people of Oakland passed a bond measure to purchase various parcels of land around Lake Merritt, which were then combined into larger green spaces that enfolded the bird refuge in a park for people. Many of the familiar lakeside attractions were built during this period, such as the pergola and colonnade along El Embarcadero. Trees were planted in Lakeside Park, but rather than focusing on native flora, as we might today, park planners wanted to include a global variety of trees so that tourists and immigrants would be able to see trees they recognized from home.

Swimming was a popular activity at Lake Merritt at this time, and a white sand beach was created as part of early efforts to market Lake Merritt as a bathing resort. Swimming was eventually deemed unsafe, though, and was banned twice, once in 1897 and again in 1912. The main issue was pollution: although the sewage issue had been resolved, a growing Oakland population still deposited plenty of pollutants into the lake (an ignominious tradition we continue to this day), and, as with the sewage, the dam restricted the lake's ability to clean itself via regular unimpeded flushing into the bay.

Despite the bans, people continued to swim in the lake for decades to follow. A story in the *Oakland Tribune* from 1932, calling for a crackdown on swimming, describes a rowdy summer scene:

> It seems that the warm afternoons and evenings have caused the youth of the Eastbay to turn to the cool waters of the lake for relief, and recreation. . . . There have been night swimming parties, au naturel, and the boys have endangered the occupants of canoes and other craft, as well as themselves, by clinging to the side of boats.

Regardless of where you stand on canoe capsizing, the ban on swimming surely helped the lake and the birds that lived on it to retain a measure of natural wildness. Similarly, the placement of booms in the 1920s to prevent boat access to certain portions of the lake, with the well-being and sanity of the ducks in mind, resulted in increases in duck populations. And, parallel with the beginnings of the environmental movement in the US, Oaklanders would start to make more of these decisions that intentionally focused on the needs and well-being of the birds, rather than their own interests, or at least that recognized that the two were intrinsically linked.

Lake Merritt Is for the Birds

Even as it was dammed and its edges landscaped, Lake Merritt remained a unique urban refuge for wild ducks and other waterbirds. Under the tutelage of local naturalist Brighton "Bugs" Cain, an early group of young Oakland bird-watchers formed the Oakland Ornithological Club in the 1930s, and published the first list of Lake Merritt birds, which put the total number of bird species that called the lake home at 138. In 1970, Paul Covel's own list had seventy-five native species. (It is unclear why the discrepancy was so wide; perhaps Covel was only counting some subset, such as waterbirds.) Some species have come and gone, such as wigeons and pintails, ducks that used to be abundant at the lake, but that now rarely (if ever) show up, due to the destruction of their nearby feeding grounds in the bay. The Lake Merritt page on the online birding platform eBird currently lists 213 species observations, though this might be from a larger geographical area than the earlier lists, as it includes numerous shorebirds that aren't typically associated with the lake. So, although the exact number of species might differ depending on whom and when you ask, the lake is no doubt home to a wide variety of birds.

Today, year-round waterbirds include Mallard ducks, pelicans, coots, gulls, cormorants, Great and Snowy Egrets, Black-crowned Night Herons (recently designated as the official bird of Oakland), Great Blue Herons, and a partial population of the sometimes contentious Canada Geese. The Pacific Flyway brings in many seasonal avian visitors as well, such as White Pelicans and grebes, and ducks such as Canvasback, Redhead, Common and Barrow's Goldeneye, Greater and Lesser Scaup, and Bufflehead. A rare Eurasian duck called a Tufted Duck, which looks like a scaup or goldeneye but with a cool ponytail, also visits occasionally, much to the excitement of local birders. During the cold and rainy winter months, the lake is brimming with these visitors; although they can be seen diving for food, they mostly just float around, with their heads tucked back into their wings as they sleep. (Duck life seems, for the most part, to be a good life.)

In the late 1800s, coinciding with the early years of the US conservation movement, the people of Oakland were beginning to take a more active interest in the birds of Lake Merritt. Ducks in particular were popular with the people, as they are the most abundant, visible, and amenable to interaction with humans. Families from all over the city and beyond would come to feed them. This was an informal pastime, and people would have to bring their own food to give to the ducks, but in 1915, an oil spill in the bay would soon change that. The oil came into the lake with the tide and coated many of Lake Merritt's ducks. The public, who had become fond of the fowl, wanted the city to help clean them up. These efforts, while well intentioned, were not very successful, and not a lot of actual cleaning took place. But a working relationship was established between humans and birds, and the public infatuation with the ducks grew.

The now somewhat oil-free ducks still needed help after this disruption to their lives, and the city council approved the allocation of funds to feed the ducks daily, making official a service that the local community had already been providing. This would prove to be a popular decision with both the ducks and the people who came to watch thousands of them flock to the twice-daily feedings, which quickly became the "city's biggest free attraction," according to park naturalist Paul Covel.

Although these feedings were initially intended as a temporary measure to help the aggrieved birds get back on their webbed feet, the mayor at the time, John L. Davie, made the policy permanent. His decision was no doubt focused on pleasing the people as much as it was on feeding the ducks: aside from the oil spill's temporary disruption, the ducks had been doing just fine and didn't need help. But Mayor Davie, who loved Lake Merritt and rowed on it daily, had taken an interest in the ducks and was determined to do more for them. His next plan would come at the risk of his own political future. He proposed a change that would forever alter the landscape of the lake and the wildlife refuge, literally, in the form of an artificial island just for ducks.

His political opponents, giddy at this perceived political misstep, termed the mayor's proposal "Davie's Folly," and were sure the public would agree with them that this was a waste of taxpayer money. Davie, a stubborn sort, proceeded with his plan anyway, and had loads of dirt shipped across the lake on barges from the site where the Kaiser Convention Center was being built. By 1923, a 20,000-square-foot island, off-limits to humans, had been created just offshore, complete with fresh water piped in for the birds to drink. The vegetation on the island was designed by landscape architect Howard Gilkey. It was proposed that the island be called Gilkey Island in his honor, but he refused and said it should be called Duck Island. (Gilkey was perhaps a more creative landscape architect than island namer.)

Whatever it was called, rather than backfiring and ending Davie's political career, Duck Island, like the public feedings, proved immensely popular. The year-round Mallard population quickly moved in to their new digs, and were able to rest, drink fresh water, and start families on the island, safe from bother by the hordes of humans on the mainland. It also provided welcome respite for the migrators arriving in the fall, who now had a safe place to land and have a drink after the long journey from their winter breeding grounds, before diving into the fray of the public feedings.

The first batch of ducks born on the island particularly captured the public's imagination: in 1924, the *Oakland Tribune* celebrated these fifteen "native-son" ducks who "no matter how far they may travel, will always return to the city of their birth." These fledglings even went on to star in a weekly radio show called *The Protective Order of Lake Merritt Ducks*, a variety show that tracked the lives of a group of fictional international ducks at the lake (and was steeped in the casual racism of the time).

There was also more serious scientific and academic interest in the lake's birds. Between the feedings and the refuge's protections, populations were burgeoning, and the US Biological Survey took interest, partnering with local businessman E. W. Ehmann for an ambitious bird-banding operation. Ehmann, a duck hunter, was interested in helping the US Biological Survey learn what they could about bird migration, life span, and more. So in 1926, bird banding began in Oakland.

Bird banding is the practice of placing small tags around the legs of birds to track their travel throughout the years. The bands are inscribed with information such as where and when the bird was tagged, and instructions for anyone finding the bird to report back to the scientific team. Little was known at the time about migratory patterns, and banding was the only way to gather this sort of information. So, in the name of science, Ehmann, park employees, boy scouts, and others got to work. One day a year, they rounded up Lake Merritt waterfowl into traps and grabbed them one by one: if the bird already had a band, its record was updated; if it didn't, a band was placed and a record created.

Initially, banding at Lake Merritt focused on the then-common pintails and wigeons, and the coot, aka mud hen, which still inhabits the lake in large quantities. A typical day might include banding as many as one or two thousand of these birds. Lake Merritt became an important node in a fledgling worldwide bird-banding network, and the birds banded at Lake Merritt were reported throughout North America and beyond.

One of these banded ducks, a particularly plucky one, might have been responsible for saving the entire operation and securing the future of the naturalist and educational programming at Lake Merritt following Mayor Davie's departure. A subsequent Oakland mayor, unimpressed with the bird protection and research activities at the lake and the amount of city resources used, threatened to cut funding. However, in 1954, seven years after the start of the Cold War, a male Northern Pintail that had been banded at Lake Merritt was recovered in enemy territory: Anabyr, Siberia. The news, and the potential thaw of Cold War hostility, was good publicity for Oakland, an aspiring international city. The mayor had a subsequent change of heart, and secured funding for wildlife refuge projects.

Toward Bringing People and Nature Together

Renewed funding and political goodwill would quickly come in handy. In 1953, the Rotary Nature Center was built on shore just across from Duck Island. It was funded mostly by donations and constructed with volunteer labor, and the final $10,000 was collected from a hesitant Oakland City Council. The modest building would soon become home to the new Oakland Park Naturalist Program.

This new center was to be led by Paul F. Covel, the first naturalist officially hired by the City of Oakland, and the first municipal naturalist anywhere in the nation. Covel, an inspired and inspiring educator, filled the new interpretive center with educational materials and taxidermy, as well as live snakes and bees, which he was convinced were the most important tools to get young children interested in and excited about nature. The daily duck feedings also helped get the attention of passersby.

Covel's book about his time at Lake Merritt, *People Are for the Birds*, paints the Lake Merritt Wildlife Refuge as an idealistic and idiosyncratic place, overflowing with passion, purpose, and potential, as well as ducks. And although ducks were the initial and primary focus of Oakland's attention at the lake, Covel knew that many other kinds of birds also called the lake home. He wanted to expand Duck Island and make it more hospitable to a wider range of feathered friends.

In the three decades after the creation of Davie's initial island folly, the refuge was expanded to include four additional islands, forming the small archipelago we are familiar with today. A wider range of plants was added to the islands, meant to more closely mimic some of the habitats that these other birds were suited to. These biodiversity efforts paid off, and almost 150 avian species, and tens of thousands of individual birds, visited the islands each year.

The next few decades would see the center continue to provide unique nature and educational experiences for Oakland residents, but shrinking budgets resulted in a gradual decline in staff. The center was almost completely closed in 1986 as the city looked for places it could cut significant chunks from its budget, but the public voiced their support, and it was saved from the chopping block. Regardless, the center continued to experience budgetary issues and was closed in 2017, ostensibly for cleaning. The Rotary Nature Center remained shuttered for almost two years, during which time there was concern it might be closed for good, before eventually reopening in 2019 (just in time for COVID-19 to shut it down again).

Other parts of the lake and estuary had been needing attention as well, and in 2002, Oakland voters passed the Measure DD bond. This bond allocated almost $200 million to Lake Merritt and estuary projects and improvements. One major change has been to reopen the channel between the lake and bay, the first stage of which was completed in 2013. The removal of the dam means that the tides can flow in and out more readily, leading to improved water quality and the ability of larger marine organisms to enter the lake, both of which are beneficial for the birds. These funds have, and still are, working to restore wetlands along the lake, enhance access by foot and bike, pay for public art to celebrate the lake, and more. Oakland locals have responded to this investment in Lake Merritt by showing up to picnic, enjoy the scenery, and commune with their nonhuman neighbors.

Although this funding has improved accessibility to the lake, the forces of exclusion, present since its founding, still exist. Samuel Merritt used the levers of power available to him as a rich, powerful white man to ban those whose use of the land he did not approve of and to increase the value of his real estate holdings. Ever-increasing real estate prices continue to act as an exclusionary force both around the lake and across Oakland. Today, rising rent prices in Oakland have contributed to a decrease in the Black population in Oakland by almost half over the past thirty years, from 43 percent in 1991 to 24 percent in 2019.

An incident in 2018 in which a white woman called the police on two Black men who were barbequing at the lake brought issues of racism, both individual and systemic, into sharp focus, and became part of a national conversation about how Black people are allowed to exist in public natural spaces. It also prompted community leaders to reclaim the lakeshore for Black people in Oakland, especially by hosting annual cookouts to celebrate "love and blackness and food and fun." While previous environmental movements have often been at odds with goals of racial equity, the modern environmental justice movement recognizes that these efforts are intrinsically linked. David Wofford, a cochair of the Rotary Nature Center Friends, a group that provides educational services at the Center, spoke of these dual concerns to the local news website *Oaklandside*: "We have the environmental community that can recognize the systemic neglect that has been applied toward the environment. And now more than ever, we're being called to recognize systemic neglect and oppression as it applies to people . . . so perhaps we can address them together."

Lake Merritt is a place where Oakland's many neighborhoods draw together and intermingle, just as the waters from the hillside creeks still stream into the once wild slough. As a waterway embedded in a city, this place needs human care and attention to keep its balance as both a refuge and a park for all. The Lake Merritt Institute, for instance, is a nonprofit that coordinates volunteers to clean up trash at the lake as well as maintain aeration fountains, which help to replenish oxygen in the water. (The EPA considers Lake Merritt an "impaired" body of water because of low oxygen levels.)

This collective stewardship of the land, in alliance with the Rotary Nature Center, extends the Center's mission "towards bringing people and nature together" at Lake Merritt. In this dawning age of climate change, and amid the ongoing fight for racial justice, fostering these community connections and this sense of stewardship will be more important than ever. Rue Mapp, a lifelong visitor to Lake Merritt's shores who has gone on to a career dedicated to connecting Black people to nature, writes of Lake Merritt:

> I think of Lake Merritt as nature's heartbeat in Oakland. The watershed that flows into and from Lake Merritt is connected to the bay and the bay is connected to the ocean. As the oldest protected watershed in the country, it is impressive that we have such important ecological history and culture right inside an urban landscape. It is also a space of refuge for birds along the Pacific Flyway to rest up for their journey ahead that also gives us, as humans, respite and regeneration for our own journeys—cookouts with family, meditative walks with friends, kayaking with children, connecting with colleagues. Lake Merritt, for me, is a place I gather and where I center myself in nature.

Lake Merritt, this little corner of the Bay Area's wetlands, our stop—for birds and humans alike—on the Pacific Flyway, one node in the network of ecosystems that make up planet Earth, will continue to be a place unique in providing us such a breadth and depth of opportunities for education, community, connection, and conservation.

Lake Merritt is a great place to start bird watching: it is easily accessible, and many of the birds are readily visible and identifiable. And it's an immersive experience: you may have to carefully avoid gulls and geese.

This guide focuses on waterbirds, but not all of the waterbirds you may encounter during a trip to Lake Merritt are included. These particular birds were chosen either because they have a special relevance to Lake Merritt or to Oakland more generally, because they are representative of a group commonly found here, or because they are fun and cool (just like you!).

If you come across birds you don't recognize, you can research them in more comprehensive field guides or by using handy computer applications such as Merlin Bird ID or online communities such as iNaturalist. Juvenile birds, hybrids, and rare visitors can often complicate the identification process, but don't fret. Embrace the mystery, and you will gain knowledge and confidence as you go. I like to focus on one or two species per trip so that I don't get overwhelmed trying to remember what color eyes a whatever-bird has or whether a juvenile so-and-so has a "short pointy beak" or a "pointy short beak." Although many of these birds can be seen along the lake's roughly three-mile perimeter of paths, the area I have found to be most conducive to spotting them stretches from Adams Point near the boathouse east to the pergola near Eastshore Park.

Go take a gander (but please don't feed the birds).

SPECIES

Black-crowned Night Heron

Nycticorax nycticorax

L 23″ – 26″

The Black-crowned Night Heron is the official bird of Oakland, though at first glance it might seem an unlikely choice for the distinction. With a black back and "crown" and big red eyes, these birds are awkward and hunched, and lack the grace of other herons. They make a sound most often called a "kwok." It was these offbeat attributes, however, that led one local third-grade class to describe the bird as "funky and cool, just like Oakland" and successfully petition the city to make the Black-crowned Night Heron the official bird of Oakland in 2019.

The most abundant of the five types of heron at the lake, these birds can be found year-round all over the area surrounding the Rotary Nature Center, islands, and duck pond; in the trees; in the water; on fences . . . anywhere and everywhere. They also roost and stride throughout the neighborhoods surrounding Lake Merritt, perhaps perching on top of a car at 5th and E. 18th Streets or standing like gargoyles on roofs and awnings along Lakeshore and Grand Avenues. Most famously, however, they can be found downtown, where they have long resisted relocation by developers who want to move or remove their rookeries to make way for new human habitats.

Although they might seem out of place in these locations, the herons are probably in exactly the same spots they have been in for thousands of years, when what is now Oakland was just a vast expanse of wetlands and rolling hills alive with coastal oaks.

Double-crested Cormorant

Phalacrocorax auritus

L 27″ – 35″

On most every visit to Lake Merritt, winter or summer, rain or shine, you're likely to see Double-crested Cormorants. These large, dark birds, with long necks and orange at the base of their long, sharp beaks, have a dinosaur-like quality. They swim low in the water when hunting, with most of their body beneath the water's surface, and seem as if they have just emerged from the lake's silty, brackish depths (which are actually only about ten feet at most). Swimming submerged like this makes it easier to catch the small fish on which they feed.

Frequently, cormorants can be spotted sunbathing, sometimes in dramatic poses, their wings flung wide in order to dry their feathers. Cormorant feathers are less oily than those of other waterbirds; waterlogged feathers enable them to dive faster and deeper, but also take longer to dry out. One good spot to see them is along the booms laid out to prevent boats from entering the water around protected areas of the lake, and another is atop the leafless trees on the islands. These trees are also the site of cormorant nests, which at first glance might look like debris hanging from the tree branches.

Double-crested Cormorants have breeding colonies throughout the Bay Area, including on the underside of both the Bay Bridge and the Richmond–San Rafael Bridge. These diffuse colonies form a "metapopulation" in which individuals move freely between sites. In 2017, cormorants started nesting in the trees above the playground near the Rotary Nature Center, and there has been speculation that these were individuals displaced by the removal of the eastern span of the old Bay Bridge, highlighting the importance of maintaining a variety of diverse breeding sites such as Lake Merritt.

American Coot

Fulica americana

L 15″ – 17″

Another year-round Lake Merritt resident is the American Coot. These birds, the size of a large cantaloupe, feed mostly by dabbling or pecking at aquatic plants and algae, sometimes diving into the shallow water to get at tasty bits below the surface. They are almost entirely a dull faded black color, with a white bill and red eyes.

Despite being one of the most common birds at Lake Merritt, the American Coot is easy to overlook. From afar, an uninterested party might see them floating about and assume they are "just ducks." (They are actually a species of rail, not even related to ducks.) It is not until you see them on land that the common American Coot becomes uncommonly interesting.

Watching birds at Lake Merritt, you can get so close to such a wide variety of wild birds that you are able to make out minute details you might otherwise only see in a photograph. And getting close to the American Coot is necessary to marvel at it, in particular at its lower limbs. A coot's feet and legs do not look as though they should be attached to their drab bodies; it's as if something got messed up at the bird assembly factory, where some chickens accidentally got outfitted with state-of-the-art aquatic bird foot technology. Their long legs extend out of their lackluster plumage, often in some shade of green, gray, blue, yellow, or orange. (The colors move toward the yellow–red spectrum as the birds age.) Their legs then flare out into three wide, flat "toes" with two to four distinct lobes each. Each lobe has a radial gradation of vibrant colors, overlaid by a black nodular mesh. This lobed look, aside from being fancy, helps the coot scoot through water as well as navigate various earthly terrains, and is even used like a snowshoe to cross the mucky mires on which they sometimes tread.

Great Blue Heron

Ardea herodias

L 38″ – 54″

The Great Blue Heron can be seen anywhere around Lake Merritt, in any season. They can also be found in the slough that feeds ocean water to the lake, the estuary to which the slough runs, in the bay, up and down California, and around the country. Indeed, the highly adaptable Great Blue Heron hunts in saltwater, freshwater, fields, and meadows, using its long yellow beak to either grab or pierce anything around. Although its mostly white head has a distinctive blue-black stripe running just above its bright yellow eyes, the easiest way to identify this bird is that it is, as the name suggests, great and blue(ish).

When I was a kid growing up in the Bay Area, the Great Blue Heron was one of the few birds that I could recognize. I must have first learned about them on an elementary school field trip to visit the celebrated Marin County naturalist Mrs. Terwilliger, who had a taxidermied one. I would often catch sight of them (neck crooked, both of us), from the backseat of the car, driving around the bay, wherever the road sat low and close alongside the water. Now, I see them at the lake. There is one particular individual who regularly stands in a specific, sunny spot on one of the docks in front of the boathouse.

Cindy Margulis, at International Bird Rescue, describes the awe of seeing Great Blue Herons in action at the lake:

> Who hasn't been excited to glimpse a Great Blue Heron nearby? Perhaps the nearly four-foot-tall bird was foraging ever so patiently for fish by the lake? Or, maybe ole GBH shocked its gawkers by gobbling a gopher all of a sudden on a patch of grass. Or maybe the Great Blue Heron was suddenly startled, and its nearly seven-foot wingspan unfurled and it took to the air? That's one of the biggest bird thrills at Lake Merritt, after all.

American White Pelican

Pelecanus erythrorhynchos

L 50" – 65"

The American White Pelican is a large, almost all-white bird, with a long yellow-orange beak and short orange legs. They have black flight feathers visible only when their wings are spread. These massive wings, nine feet across, propel groups of migrating pelicans far and wide throughout North and Central America, heading north to inland lakes in the spring to breed, and south to coastal waters, such as Lake Merritt, in the winter.

But when Hank the pelican showed up at the lake in 2004, she was alone. Hank is an American White Pelican who initially came to the refuge after her wing was injured in a collision with a power line around Klamath Falls, Oregon. Naturalists there called around to find someone to take care of her, and the Lake Merritt Wildlife Refuge, which had previously taken care of two other injured American White Pelicans (Hector and Helen in the 1980s and 1990s), agreed to take her. But at the time, no other pelicans had been recently wintering at the lake. These birds are social hunters, meaning they work together, and with a bum wing and no friends, Hank was not able to fish on her own. One employee of the wildlife refuge recounted that he would take regular trips into Oakland's Chinatown to buy tilapia for Hank to eat.

After Hank had been at the lake for three or so years, another white pelican stopped here during migration, likely after spotting Hank. Two more came the next year, and now it is not uncommon for ten or twenty of these pelicans to visit in a season. These days, seeing American White Pelicans is a common occurrence at Lake Merritt, at least during the migratory season from September to February. If you happen to see one outside of those months, it's probably Hank!

Canada Goose

Branta canadensis

L 30" – 43"

Canada Geese are perhaps the easiest bird to spot at Lake Merritt, and for human visitors it is as much an issue of avoiding them as it is of identifying them. They are recognizable by their black head and neck, white chin, and brown body. They are large, loud, and probably blocking the path and pooping all over the grass. There is a year-round population of a few hundred geese, but their numbers can balloon to over two thousand during the summer months.

These geese used to be regular visitors to the area during their seasonal migration, but they stopped coming once the lake was dammed up and the edges paved over. When Paul Covel became the park naturalist, he was, as he wrote in his book *People Are for the Birds*, "determined to build up a flock of these desirable birds," which he appreciated for their ability to coexist with humans: "The Canada goose accepts man, his man-made habitats, and his protection." An opportunity to reintroduce geese to the lake presented itself when a farmer from the nearby Sacramento Valley called and asked if Lake Merritt would be interested in taking some of the geese off of his land. Covel and a few others went and came back with nine geese, two of whom happened to be a mating pair that would be the start of a regular population of Canada Geese at Lake Merritt.

As the goose population has grown, so has the number of complaints that the city receives about them, both about their behavior and their impact on the local ecosystem. So, as part of improving the lake thanks to Measure DD, the city has studied the challenges of "goose management." Oakland's approach has been a case in point of what makes the wildlife refuge at Lake Merritt so valuable: that it encourages us to strive to be thoughtful and careful in finding ways to coexist with our avian neighbors or, as the study puts it, "balance the needs of lake and park users with the grazing and habitat needs of the Canada goose population."

Green Heron

Butorides virescens

L 16" – 18"

Green Herons are a more elusive counterpart to the louder and more numerous Black-crowned Night Herons, preferring to stalk the lake's periphery from the cover of bushes and low-hanging branches, where they patiently await unaware fish. They have been known to use a lure, such as a breadcrumb or insect, to attract fish while they hunt, placing these birds among the few known for using tools. Mostly a green and dark gray with a reddish-brown neck, dark beak, and orange or yellow eyes and legs, their coloration lends particularly well to camouflage among the dappled vegetative underbrush in which they lurk.

This heron's stealthy behavior and camouflage can make it hard to spot, but when your senses are alert and if there's a bit of serendipity, you might have an encounter like that of writer and artist—and attentive Lake Merritt bird-watcher—Jenny Odell:

> The first time I ever saw a Green Heron was in the Botanical Garden, by the pond with all the turtles. I was sitting on a bench looking into this green space, and it was right in front of me. The Green Heron. Super blended in with everything. It's weird when you know what a bird is from a book and then you see it in real life. And it was so still. I thought, *Am I actually seeing this?* It was doing the bird version of licking its lips. I saw its tongue slide along its beak. It was surreal. Such a strange creature. I sat staring at it for a really long time. Every time I go back to that garden now, I forlornly stand near the pond hoping that I'll see it again, but it's never happened again.

So if you are having some difficulty spotting a Green Heron at the lake and are tired of "scouring the underbrush," try *not* looking for one and see if that works!

Snowy Egret

Egretta thula

L 22" – 26"

The bright white Snowy Egret stands out against the murky edges of the lake where it hunts. They are slender, medium-size birds with long, spindly black legs ending in bright yellow feet. Their beaks are sharp black points with a bright yellow patch at the base. Sometimes mistaken for another white egret, the Great Egret, which is also found at Lake Merritt, the two species can be differentiated by size (Great Egrets are much larger) and beak and foot coloration. (Great Egrets' coloring is reversed: black feet and an all-yellow beak.)

Scientists have described thirty-four unique hunting behaviors in herons (egrets are a type of heron) with fun and descriptive names such as foot probing, dipping, leapfrog feeding, and underwing-feeding. Snowy Egrets have been known to utilize twenty-one of these behaviors, the most of any North American heron. Lake Merritt is a great place to observe this wide array of behaviors, with these birds seemingly unbothered by humans walking along the raised pathways just a few feet away from them. While they sometimes stay statue still, peaceful and serene (or is that the hunting behavior called "standing"?), they can often be found frantically combing the muck, looking for fish. Their bright yellow feet can make it easy to see them actively disturbing the muddy bottom, although perhaps only a trained eye will be able to differentiate between foot-stirring, foot-raking, foot probing, and foot paddling.

Although Snowy Egret populations have rebounded, and even expanded, since they were nearly wiped out by hunters in the late 1800s, they are still threatened by habitat loss as wetlands disappear across the country. This risk played out locally in vivid detail in 2019 when a large tree fell in downtown Oakland that was home to between fifty and one hundred Snowy Egret and Black-crowned Night Heron nests. Numerous local organizations worked together to rescue, rehabilitate, and release the young birds back into the wild, demonstrating the need to continue protecting the places that allow these birds to thrive.

Western Grebe

Aechmophorus occidentalis

L 21" – 29"

Western Grebes are one of five types of grebe that spend time at Lake Merritt, where they can be found diving beneath the surface in pursuit of their fish dinners. The grebe's pointy yellow beak pokes out from a black hood that is connected to its sooty body by a wide black stripe down the back of a long, otherwise white neck. Once considered to be the same species as the Clark's Grebe, the main differentiator is that the Clark's wears its hat on its head like folks normally do, while the Western Grebe has pulled it down over its eyes and cut out eye holes like a superhero mask, the black extending beneath its eyes. They spend almost all their time in the water and are not much good at walking on land due to their feet being placed so far back on their bodies. When they do find themselves ashore, they stagger like a drunken tap dancer.

Western Grebes spend the cold fall and winter months vacationing along the coast, traveling north and east during the spring to their breeding grounds at inland lakes. California lakes such as Clear Lake, north of Napa, can see thousands of them nesting and breeding during the summer breeding season, where they perform extravagant courtship rituals such as running in tandem across the lake's surface, a behavior commonly known as "water dancing." They also have another mating dance called the "weed ceremony" (insert stoner laugh) in which a pair will bring up weeds from the bottom of a lake and excitedly present them to each other. These behaviors make them one of the more entertaining and remarkable birds to search for among the reeds and ponds of the internet, if you can't make it up to Clear Lake anytime soon.

Here at Lake Merritt, their long, slender necks help them stand out from the crowd of stubbier ducks and coots.

Greater Scaup

Aythya marila

L 15" – 22"

Much of Lake Merritt's history as a wildlife refuge has been duck-centric: the first island was called Duck Island; there were the popular daily duck feedings and the bird-banding operations focused on ducks; and in 2020, a pair of abandoned domestic ducks made headlines after surviving on a drainpipe at the edge of the lake.

Although the exact species that frequent the lake have changed over time, you can always count on seeing large rafts of ducks floating idly on the lake in the winter months, when migratory ducks move south, away from their cold northern breeding grounds to the warmer winter waters of Oakland. And one of the more numerous ducks you might see these days is also the species that travels the farthest to get here, the Greater Scaup; their breeding grounds are in the tundra above the Arctic Circle!

Male Greater Scaups are one of a few types of duck often described as "Oreo ducks" thanks to a dark head, breast, and tail, which sandwich a white midsection that's gray on top. (If your Oreo's white midsection is gray on top, consider not eating it.) Up close, you might notice that this gray color is an intricate black-and-white striping, reminiscent of the "flyknit" Nike shoe fabric. Yes, this duck resembles a cross between a running shoe and a delicious cookie treat. Its head is round and can have a slight green sheen, which, among other fairly inscrutable differences, differentiates it from the also common Lesser Scaup, who has a pointier head and purple sheen. (If your Oreo has a slight green or purple sheen, consider not eating it.)

As is often the case with ducks, males are more colorful and easily recognizable than females. Female Greater Scaups are mostly a mottled brown (think molasses cookie) and have a darker brown head with white around the bill and pale spots on their cheeks. Both male and female have yellow eyes and beautiful silvery blue beaks from which they derive their "bluebill" nickname.

Canvasback Duck

Aythya valisineria

L 19" – 22"

Canvasbacks are another diving duck that migrates to Lake Merritt for the winter, coming south from the marshes where they breed in Alaska, the Yukon, and Alberta, Canada. Shy around humans, these ducks are most readily found offshore, toward the center of the lake.

A few more obvious indicators of a Canvasback are its size, larger than most of the ducks around it, and the male's bright off-white ("canvas") back, which stands out among the other ducks and against the blue-gray waters on which they all float. Males have a rich red-brown head; intense, kind of creepy red eyes; and a black beak, breast, and tail. Female Canvasbacks have a rich, almost caramel head, neck, and tail, with a pale body and dark eyes and beak. Both males and females have a long beak and sloping forehead, which make them look roughly like a hand inside a Canvasback sock puppet.

While you might see only modest numbers of Canvasbacks at Lake Merritt, or throughout the California coast in general, there were once huge flocks of them throughout the state. (A Spanish map from 1775 referred to the northern Bay Area marshes as the "forests of the red duck.") However, the throngs of gold miners who started arriving in California in the mid-nineteenth century needed something to eat, and hunting soon became a very popular secondary activity to mining. The large Canvasbacks, considered to be one of the tastier birds, were easy targets. Market hunters developed methods by which to kill many birds at once, such as the "punt gun" (really more like a cannon), which could kill over fifty in a single shot, and the advent of refrigerated train cars vastly expanded the available market. In 1910, over half a million ducks of all kinds were sold in San Francisco alone. The resulting decline in bird populations was obvious and caused a backlash from an increasingly environmentally focused public, including sport hunters interested in maintaining sustainable populations to hunt.

Common Goldeneye

Bucephala clangula

L 16″ – 20″

In her book *A Wizard of Earthsea*, East Bay native Ursula K. Le Guin writes, "A mage can control only what is near him, what he can name exactly and wholly." While knowing the name of the Common Goldeneye will not necessarily make you a mage or give you control over these migratory, medium-size diving ducks, there is still something of a thrill to be had in being able to identify and differentiate between the three types of goldeneye, two of which are ducks and one of which is a James Bond movie. (Fun fact: the creator of James Bond, Ian Fleming, was an avid birder, and named his protagonist after an American ornithologist.)

Once you spot a goldeneye, the first step in identification is to ascertain whether you are looking at a 1995 spy film starring Pierce Brosnan. If so, you are probably watching Martin Campbell's *Golden-Eye*. If not, you are probably looking at a duck that is either a Common or a Barrow's Goldeneye. But how to tell the difference between these two doppelgänger ducks?

If you are looking at a female, you might have trouble, as the two species are almost identical: gray bodies with a rich brown head. (Their bill can sometimes provide a clue, at least in the colder months: mostly yellow for Barrow's and mostly black for Common.) Males are also very similar: black head, short black beak, and a white body with black wings and tail, but the one major tell is a minor difference in the shape of a prominent white spot on the cheek. The Common's is round or slightly oval shaped, whereas the Barrow's is more of a teardrop or crescent shape. There are a few other minor differences, such as in head sheen (green on the Common, purple on the Barrow's, Estevez in the Mighty Ducks), and in wing color pattern. But for the most part, it's just the cheek thing.

Ruddy Duck

Oxyura jamaicensis

L 14″ – 17″

One of the lake's more miniature migrators, the Ruddy Duck can primarily be found during the winter and winter-adjacent months. "Ruddy" refers to the red color that the male takes on during the breeding season, although they are more likely to be "muddy" ducks at Lake Merritt, with a dull gray-brown coloration during the winter. Females are dull brown year-round. Their bright white cheeks (with a stripe of brown across in females) can help with identification. They feed at night, so you might see them resting during the day with their head tucked back cozily into a wing, but just because they can't see you doesn't mean you can't see them!

Clayton Anderson of the Golden Gate Audubon Society says of the Ruddy Duck:

> This little chunky red brick of a bird has been known by many names. When disturbed, this duck prefers to swim away or dive, rather than fly, to avoid danger. Unfortunately, this means that when the duck is facing humans with guns, hunters have plenty of time to reload and fire again when it resurfaces. Ruddy Ducks are also sometimes called the Bobbler, Dipper, Dip-tailed Diver, Ruddy Diver, and Sinker, because they swim underwater to find their food. Therefore, if you want to see the beauty of the Ruddy, you'll generally need binoculars to see them out in the middle of the deep pools.

If you don't have binoculars or the light is low and you can only make out birds' silhouettes, try looking for stiff tail feathers sticking up and out from their rears, a Ruddy Duck signature look.

Glaucous-winged Gull

Larus glaucescens

L 19″ – 23″

Are you getting tired of constantly seeing gulls at Lake Merritt and never knowing which kind of gull it is you are looking at? Did one of them steal your sandwich and you want to know whether it was a Glaucous-winged Gull or some other gull that did the dirty deed? Well, look no further. Here at *Birds of Lake Merritt* we know one weird trick that is guaranteed to help you identify the Glaucous-winged Gull right on time, every time:*

Step one: Look at its wing.

Step two: Is it glaucous?

If your answer to step two is yes, congratulations, you might be dealing with a Glaucous-winged Gull.** But what *is* "glaucous"? you might be thinking (or Googling because you are impatient). Well, it's another word for *gray*. So, basically, these gulls look like all the other types of gulls at the lake, of which there are many, except that their wings are gray. "But wait," you yell, eliciting sidelong glances from anyone around you, "don't many gulls have gray wings?" Yes they do, but the Glaucous-winged Gull's wings are gray all the way down to the wingtips, whereas on other gulls the wingtips are black or white. So, in summary, if you see a gull that has gray wingtips, you, my friend, might be looking at a Glaucous-winged Gull.***

Keep an eye out for these, and other gulls, flying high and dropping clams and mussels onto the concrete paths below, cracking the shell to get at their tender innards.

*Results not guaranteed; identifying gulls is actually pretty intense and difficult. Offer only valid from late September to early May, when Glaucous-winged Gulls come south for the winter. Void where prohibited.

**It might also be a Glaucous Gull . . . a tale for another time.

***Unless it's an "Olympic Gull," which is not really a unique species but a hybrid between a Glaucous-winged Gull and a Western Gull. It also has gray wingtips but . . . less gray.

Belted Kingfisher

Megaceryle alcyon

L 11″ – 14″

These are small, stocky birds with big beaks, crested blue heads, and blue bodies with a white neck and belly. Females wear a dashing rust-colored "belt" across their front. While many waterbirds spend their time primarily *on* the water, some, like the Belted Kingfisher, spend their time mostly around and above it, dipping in only when hunting. They often look as though they went out the night before and slicked their hair back but didn't wash out the mousse before going to bed, which they do in earthen burrows adjacent to the bodies of water where they feed. These burrows are three to six feet deep, and they dig them with their beaks . . . not bad for a little bird! You might hear the Belted Kingfisher before you see it: it has a loud call like a quick, vibrating "e-e-e-e" sound, almost like a rattle.

Or so I have been led to believe by my research. For I must admit that I have not positively identified a Belted Kingfisher at Lake Merritt. I have listened for them beyond the noise of nearby traffic and studied photos on iNaturalist to find out where they have been spotted previously (on branches over the water, sometimes atop lampposts). I have read about their habitat and behavior, and even got drunk at the Kingfish bar (unrelated) on Telegraph—good Palomas, but no luck.

Choosing to paint them was aspirational, almost an invocation, as if I could summon one by replicating its likeness. But it turns out that isn't the way it works. Nor has painstakingly detailing their plumage helped me identify them as they zip through the trees. I have seen birds that I think *might* be a kingfisher, but, dang it, I just can't be sure. I am sure I'll track one down eventually, and I'll be excited when I do. But in the meantime, I am enjoying the process and anticipation, and have an excuse for another bike ride along the lake's edge.

REFERENCES AND BIBLIOGRAPHY

GENERAL BIBLIOGRAPHY

Anderson, M. Kat. *Tending the Wild*. Berkeley: University of California Press, 2005.

Billerman, Shawn, Brooke Keeney, Paul Rodewald, and Tom Schulenberg, eds. Birds of the World. Ithaca, NY: Cornell Laboratory of Ornithology. https://birdsoftheworld.org/bow/home.

Cornell Lab of Ornithology. All About Birds. https://www.allaboutbirds.org.

Cornell Lab of Ornithology. eBird [Online database of bird distribution and abundance]. http://www.ebird.org.

Covel, Paul F. *People Are for the Birds*. Oakland, CA: Western Interpretive Press, 1978.

iNaturalist. https://www.inaturalist.org.

INTRODUCTION

References

"'With their parallel lives . . .'": Berger, John. *Why Look at Animals?* London: Penguin, 2009, 6. Originally published in 1977.

"He confronts Muir's vision": Burress, Rex. "Letter to John Muir." *California Parks and Recreation*, November 1962. https://vault.sierraclub.org/john_muir_exhibit/life/burress_ltr_to_muir.aspx.

"But perhaps a lake can be more of a state of mind": Hampl, Patricia. "Lake." In *Home Ground: A Guide to the American Landscape*, edited by Barry Lopez and Debra Gwartney. San Antonio, TX: Trinity University Press, 2006, 262.

On the history of the Ohlone at Lake Merritt: Gould, Corrina. In
    Noonan, Katie, David Wofford, and John Kirkmire. "Lake Mer-
    ritt Wildlife Refuge 150th Anniversary." YouTube video, 1:20:00,
    September 16, 2020. https://www.youtube.com/watch?v=
    c8sYscREWws.

Samuel Merritt on his first visit to Oakland: *Oakland Tribune*, April
    5, 1884. Quoted in Bagwell, Beth. *Oakland: The Story of a City*.
    Novato, CA: Presidio Press, 1982, 17.

On the hunting scene at Lake Merritt and Covel's 1970 list of bird
    species: Young, John V. "A Doctor's Tonic for Oakland Birds."
    New York Times, April 12, 1970. https://www.nytimes
    .com/1970/04/12/archives/a-doctors-tonic
    -for-oakland-birds.html.

Oakland founding Lake Merritt as a public park: "M. C. Chapman
    Lauded at Public Fete." *Oakland Tribune*, September 6, 1930, C13.

Lake Merritt as a point of civic pride: *Oakland Daily Evening Tribune*,
    Special Illustrated Edition, January 20, 1887. Quoted in Bagwell,
    Beth. *Oakland: The Story of a City*. Novato, CA: Presidio Press,
    1982, 123.

On the summer scene at Lake Merritt: "Public Issue Ban on Swim-
    ming in Lake Merritt." *Oakland Tribune*, July 27, 1932, 4C.

"The first batch of ducks born on the island": "Born, on Island in
    Lake Merritt, 15 Native-Son Ducks." *Oakland Tribune*, April 23,
    1924, 11.

On the loss of Oakland's Black population: Markovich, Ally. "A
    New Film Celebrates Lake Merritt's 150th Anniversary as the
    Nation's First Wildlife Refuge." *Oaklandside*, October 21, 2020.
    https://oaklandside.org/2020/10/21/a-new-film-celebrates-lake
    -merritts-150th-anniversary-as-the-nations-first-wildlife-refuge/.

On celebrating "love and blackness and food and fun": Holson, Laura
    M. "Hundreds in Oakland Turn Out to BBQ While Black."
    New York Times, May 21, 2018. https://www.nytimes
    .com/2018/05/21/us/oakland-bbq-while-black.html.

David Wofford on environmental justice: Markovich, Ally. "A New
    Film Celebrates Lake Merritt's 150th Anniversary as the Nation's
    First Wildlife Refuge." *Oaklandside*, October 21, 2020. https://

oaklandside.org/2020/10/21/a-new-film-celebrates-lake
-merritts-150th-anniversary-as-the-nations-first-wildlife-refuge/.
Rue Mapp writing about Lake Merritt: Mapp, Rue. Email message to
the author, November 12, 2020.

Bibliography

Bagwell, Beth. *Oakland: The Story of a City*. Novato, CA: Presidio
Press, 1982.

Beatley, Timothy. *The Bird-Friendly City*. Washington, DC: Island
Press, 2020.

Beery, Zoë. "The Long, Complex History of Oakland's Man-Made
Bird Islands." Atlas Obscura, March 8, 2018. https://www
.atlasobscura.com/articles/lake-merritt-bird-islands-oakland.

Benavidez, Stephanie. "Lake Merritt Bird Sanctuary." Audio file.
Interview by Michael Fitzhugh. Internet Archive, March 2005.
https://archive.org/details/MichaelFitzhughLakeMerrittBird-
Sanctuary.

Covel, Paul F. *Beacons along a Naturalist's Trail*. Oakland, CA: Western Interpretive Press, 1988.

Davie, John L. *His Honor, the Buckaroo: The Autobiography of John L.
Davie*. Reno, NV: Jack Herzberg, 1988.

Eaton, Joe. "Tallying Bird Populations Then and Now." *San Francisco
Estuary*, December 2020. https://www.sfestuary.org
/estuary-news-tallying-waterfowl/.

Fibel, Pearl Randolph. *The Peraltas*. Oakland, CA: Peralta Hospital,
1971.

George, Aleta. "Conservationists Who Hunt Describe Their Connection to Nature." *Bay Nature*, October-December 2014.
https://baynature.org/article/view-blind-hunters-take-aim-con-
servation/.

Heinitz, John. "The Early Development of Lake Merritt, Oakland,
California: 1852–1907." Master's thesis. California State University, Hayward, 1992.

Jordan, Harriet. "Public Parks, 1885–1914." *Garden History* 22, no. 1
(Summer 1994): 85–113. https://www.jstor.org

/stable/1587004?seq=1.

Kerr, Dara. "Lake Merritt's Nature Center Continues on Despite Budget Cuts." *Oakland North*, September 6, 2010. https://oaklandnorth.net/2010/09/06/lake-merritts-nature-center-continues-on-despite-budget-cuts/.

Koford, Henning. *Dr. Samuel Merritt: His Life and Achievements.* Oakland, CA: Kennedy Co. Printers, 1938.

Margolin, Malcolm. *The Ohlone Way.* Berkeley, CA: Heyday, 1978.

Marshall, Amelia Sue. *East Bay Hills: A Brief History.* Charleston, SC: History Press, 2017.

McFerrin, Linda Watanabe. "A Natural History of Oakland's Lake Merritt." *Bay Nature*, January–March 2001. https://baynature.org/article/loving-lake-merritt/.

Miller, Cheryl. "Identifying, Evaluating and Managing a Historic Landscape: A Case Study of Lake Merritt." Master's thesis. University of California, Berkeley, 1983.

Morris, Scott. "What Ever Happened to the Rotary Nature Center?" *East Bay Express*, February 2018. https://www.eastbayexpress.com/oakland/what-ever-happened-to-the-rotary-nature-center/Content?oid=13051780.

Noonan, Katie, David Wofford, and John Kirkmire. "Lake Merritt Wildlife Refuge 1870–2020 – 150th Anniversary Celebration Program." YouTube video, 1:41:29, October 26, 2020, https://www.youtube.com/watch?v=nXVPkhsq5yg.

Oakland Wiki, s.v. "Lake Merritt History." Last modified March 9, 2016, 17:13. https://localwiki.org/oakland/Lake_Merritt_History.

———, s.v. "Lake Merritt Wild Duck Refuge." Last modified March 18, 2020, 12:30. https://localwiki.org/oakland/Lake_Merritt_Wild_Duck_Refuge.

O'Donoghue, Liam. "Exploring Lake Merritt and Children's Fairyland." *East Bay Yesterday.* Podcast audio. April 25, 2019. https://eastbayyesterday.com/episodes/eby-qa/.

Ortega-Welch, Marissa. "Birding Hotspot: Lake Merritt." (Blog post). Golden Gate Audubon Society, n.d. https://goldengateaudubon.org/blog-posts/birding-hotspot-lake-merritt/.

———. "This Lake Is for the Birds: Stories from the Nation's First Wildlife Refuge." *KALW*, March 17, 2020. https://www

.kalw.org/post/lake-birds-stories-nation-s-first-wildlife-refuge
#stream/0.

Parrish, Will. "Living on Ohlone Land." *East Bay Express*, May 30,
2018. https://m.eastbayexpress.com/oakland
/living-on-ohlone-land/Content?oid=16512595.

Price, Jennifer. *Flight Maps*. New York: Basic Books, 1999.

Terplan, Egon, and Magda Maaoi. "Four Plans That Shaped Downtown Oakland's First 100 Years." *Urbanist*, February 3, 2015.
https://www.spur.org/publications/urbanist-article/2015-02-03
/four-plans-shaped-downtown-oakland-s-first-100-years.

SPECIES

Black-crowned Night Heron

Lefebvre, Sam. "Is Oakland Failing Its Official Bird?" *Oaklandside*,
August 4, 2020. https://oaklandside.org/2020/08/04
/oakland-save-official-bird-night-heron-developers/.

Ortega-Welch, Marissa. "Will Oakland's Herons Ever Leave Downtown for a New Home at Lake Merritt?" *KALW*, April 4, 2019.
https://www.kalw.org/post/will-oaklands-herons-ever-leave-down
town-new-home-lake-merritt#stream/0.

Double-crested Cormorant

Noonan, Katie. "Cormorants Colonize the Mainland at Lake Merritt." *Tidings*, no. 6 (2017): 1.

Rauzon, Mark J., Meredith L. Elliott, Phillip J. Capitolo, L. Max
Tarjan, Gerard J. McChesney, John P. Kelly, and Harry R.
Carter. "Changes in Abundance and Distribution of Nesting
Double-Crested Cormorants Phalacrocorax Auritus in the San
Francisco Bay Area, 1975–2017." *Marine Ornithology* 47 (2019):127–38.

Great Blue Heron

Cindy Margulis on seeing Great Blue Herons: Margulis, Cindy. Electronic communication with author via LinkedIn, December 3, 2020.

American White Pelican

On park employees feeding Hank: Cole, Timothy. Interview with the author, 2020.

Bay Area News Group. "White Pelicans Flock to Lake Merritt Wildlife Refuge to Greet Hank." *East Bay Times*, October 25, 2013. https://www.eastbaytimes.com/2013/10/25/white-pelicans-flock -to-lake-merritt-wildlife-refuge-to-greet-hank/.

Canada Goose

Jones & Stokes Associates. "Lake Merritt Canada Goose Management Study." Prepared for the City of Oakland. July 2007. http://www2.oaklandnet.com/w/OAK036286.

Green Heron

On her encounter with a Green Heron: Odell, Jenny. Interview with the author, May 14, 2020.

Snowy Egret

Garvin, Alison. "Takes a Village . . . To Save a Colony!" (Blog post). Golden Gate Audubon Society, July 2019. https://goldenga-teaudubon.org/blog-posts/takes-a-village-to-save-a-colony/.

Canvasback

Hart, John. "Canvasback." *Bay Nature*, July–September 2007. https://baynature.org/article/canvasback/.

Hickman, David, and Don Morrill. "Market Hunting in the Yolo Basin, 1850–1950." *Yolo Flyway* 21, no. 1 (Winter 2012): 1–4. http://

yolobasin.org/wp-content/uploads/PDF/yfnl/ybf_flyway_2012
_winter.pdf.

Common Goldeneye

Pierce, Ted. "Barrow's Goldeneye at Lake Merritt." *Gull* 73, no. 4
    (April 1991): 67–69. https://archive.org/details/gull7341gold
    /mode/2up.
Sibley, David. "Distinguishing Female Barrow's and Common
    Goldeneyes." (Blog post). *Sibley Guides*, January 2010. https://
    www.sibleyguides.com/2010/01/distinguishing-female-bar-
    rows-and-common-goldeneyes/.

Ruddy Duck

Description of the Ruddy Duck: Anderson, Clayton. Email message
    to the author, January 25, 2021.

Glaucous-winged Gull

Maron, John L. "Shell Dropping Behavior of Western Gulls (*Larus
    Occidentalis*)." *Auk* 99 (July 1982): 565–569. https://sora.unm
    .edu/sites/default/files/journals/auk/v099n03/p0565-p0569.pdf.

About the Author

Alex Harris, born and raised in Berkeley, California, is an artist interested in using art and technology to look at how humans interface with the natural world. He has a BA in environmental studies from the University of California, Santa Cruz, and previously worked as the web editor and electronic communications manager at the Berkeley Art Museum and Pacific Film Archive. He lives and works in Oakland, California. More information is available online at alexharris.art.